Friendship Warms the Heart

A Special Gift

To

_____

From

_____

Date

Little Ribbons of Love

A Little Book of Christmas Joy
Afternoon Tea · Angels: Ever in Our Midst
Classics of the Heart
Friendship Warms the Heart · Flowers for a Friend
Kittens: Discovering the Joys of Life
Rose Garden Memories
Sisters: So Much We Share

Friendship Warms the Heart

Brownlow

Brownlow Publishing Company, Inc.

Friendships
link and loop
and interweave
until they
mesh the world.

PAM BROWN

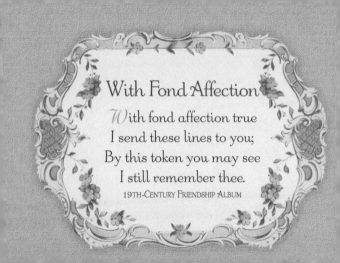

With Fond Affection

With fond affection true
I send these lines to you;
By this token you may see
I still remember thee.

19TH-CENTURY FRIENDSHIP ALBUM

Friendship and Love

The thread of our life would be dark,
Heaven knows!
If it were not with friendship and love
intertwin'd.

THOMAS MOORE

Peace

Peace to you.
The friends here send
their greetings.
Greet the friends there by name.

3 JOHN 14

When you
love someone all
your saved up wishes
start coming out.

ELIZABETH BOWEN

A Little Secret

There's a little secret
Worth its weight in gold,
Easy to remember
Easy to be told;

Changing into blessing
Every curse we meet,
Turning earth to heaven;
This is all: Keep sweet!

A. B. SIMPSON

*M*ake the attempt if you want to,
but you will find that trying to go
through life without friendship is
like milking a bear to get cream
for your morning coffee. It is a
whole lot of trouble, and then not
worth much after you get it.

ZORA NEALE HURSTON

The Flower of Love

Love is like a beautiful flower
which I may not touch,
but whose fragrance makes
the garden a place of delight
just the same.

HELEN KELLER

*Much happiness is overlooked
because it doesn't cost anything.*

OSCAR WILDE

*Love demands infinitely less
than friendship.*

GEORGE JEAN NATHAN

God gave me a friend. At once
I felt within my soul the stir of
nobler depths. As if with one touch
He woke a hidden spring that rose
to joyous being. Two souls as one
became, and heart to heart we spoke
in perfect unison. And thence
from each went out an endless

flow of love to all mankind,
in thankfulness to Him who, knowing
all, had drawn one to the other.
I cry for joy! God gave me a friend!

AUTHOR UNKNOWN

*L*et us open up our natures, throw
wide the doors of our hearts and let in
the sunshine of good will and kindness.

O. S. MARDEN

*T*he highest heavens belong
to the Lord, but the earth
he has given to man.

PSALM 115:16

*Faith is an activity;
it is something
that has
to be applied.*

CORRIE TEN BOOM

Learn to
hold loosely
all that is not
eternal.

AGNES MAUD ROYDEN

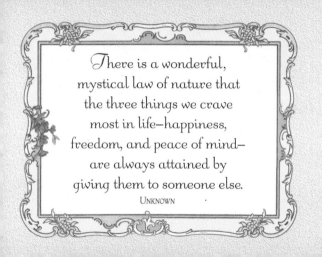

There is a wonderful,
mystical law of nature that
the three things we crave
most in life—happiness,
freedom, and peace of mind—
are always attained by
giving them to someone else.

UNKNOWN

Tears and Laughter

At my table, sit with me.
I'll pour coffee or some tea;
Perhaps we'll share
our tears and laughter
And be friends forever after.

*L*istening is a magnetic
and strange thing, a creative force.
The friends who listen to us are
the ones we move toward, and we
want to sit in their radius. When
we are listened to, it creates us,
makes us unfold and expand.

KARL MENNINGER

May the righteous be glad and rejoice before God; may they be happy and joyful.

PSALM 68:3

*Make happy
those who are near,
and those who are
far will come.*

CHINESE PROVERB

Lose no
chance of
giving
pleasure.

Frances R. Havergal

This world is but the vestibule
of eternity. Every good thought
or deed touches a chord that
vibrates in heaven.
ANONYMOUS

They serve God well
who serve His creatures.
CAROLINE NORTON

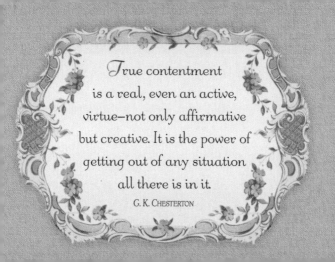

*True contentment
is a real, even an active,
virtue—not only affirmative
but creative. It is the power of
getting out of any situation
all there is in it.*

G. K. CHESTERTON

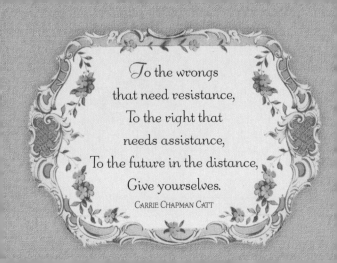

To the wrongs
that need resistance,
To the right that
needs assistance,
To the future in the distance,
Give yourselves.

CARRIE CHAPMAN CATT

My best friend
is the one
who brings out
the best in me.

HENRY FORD

A Tender Song

What's friendship but the sweetness
Of an olden, tender song
A fondness that remembers
A little kindness long.

What's life without a friendship
That time has proven true!
And all the cheer and comfort
That I have found in you.

H.J.M.

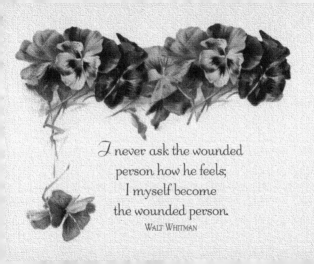

I never ask the wounded
person how he feels;
I myself become
the wounded person.

WALT WHITMAN

When friends stop being
frank and useful to each other,
the whole world loses
some of its radiance.

ANATOLE BROYARD

I will sing to the Lord, for he has been good to me.

PSALM 13:6

*W*hat wealth it is to have such friends that we cannot think of them without elevation.

HENRY DAVID THOREAU

Friendship, like love, must be largely taken "for better or for worse." It is idle to "throw over" a friend who in many ways gives you pleasant and agreeable companionship, because, indeed, you discover faults not at first perceived. If one waits to find perfection in his friend, he will probably wait long and die unfriended at last.

*Anyone with a
heart full of friendship
has a hard time
finding enemies.*

Friendship's Garden

In my Friendship Garden
Grows a flower rare and true.
I look a little closer
And find that it is you.

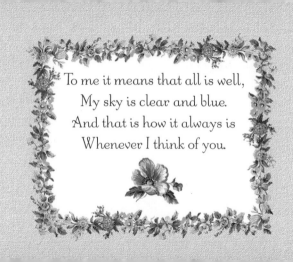

To me it means that all is well,
My sky is clear and blue.
And that is how it always is
Whenever I think of you.

*W*hen one door of
happiness closes, another opens;
but often we look so long
at the closed door that we
do not see the one which
has been opened for us.

HELEN KELLER

A Touch of Mercy

Teach me to feel another's woe,
To hide the fault I see;
That mercy I to others show,
That mercy show to me.

ALEXANDER POPE

$Love$ God completely.
Love others compassionately.
Love yourself correctly.

Anonymous

For everything that lives is holy;
life delights in life.

William Blake

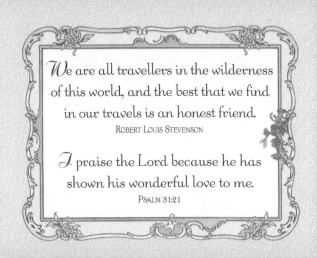

We are all travellers in the wilderness of this world, and the best that we find in our travels is an honest friend.

ROBERT LOUIS STEVENSON

I praise the Lord because he has shown his wonderful love to me.

PSALM 31:21

Treat your friends as you do your
picture, and place them in their best light.

JENNIE JEROME CHURCHILL

Friendship is a word,
the very sight of which in print
makes the heart warm.

AUGUSTINE BIRRELL

The only time to look down on
your neighbor is when you are
bending over to help.

It is almost impossible to smile
on the outside without feeling better
on the inside.

When I think of those who have
influenced my life the most, I think
not of the great but of the good.

JOHN KNOX

A friend is the gift of God,
and He only who made hearts
can unite them.

ROBERT SOUTHEY

*G*ood character, like good soup,
is made at home.

ANONYMOUS

*C*heerfulness is the atmosphere
in which all things thrive.

JOHANN PAUL RICHTER

There will be peace in the
world so far as there is
righteousness in the heart.

JOHN MILLER

A friend warms the heart.

ANONYMOUS

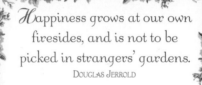

Happiness grows at our own firesides, and is not to be picked in strangers' gardens.

DOUGLAS JERROLD

A friendless man is like a left hand without a right.

PROVERB

With Those We Love

To be with those we love is enough.
Ah, how true it is! and it is a
happiness which will outlast this
life. In this thought I love to rest.

MADAME SWETCHINE

Friendship is a spiritual thing.
It is independent of matter or
space or time. That which I love in
my friend is not that which I see.
What influences me in my friend
is not his body, but his spirit.

JOHN DRUMMOND

May the Lord bless you

and keep you;

the Lord make his face shine

upon you and be gracious to you;

the Lord turn his face toward you

and give you peace.

Numbers 6:24-26

It is one mark of a friend that he
makes you wish to be at your best
while you are with him.

HENRY VAN DYKE

It is always wise to stop wishing
for things long enough to enjoy the
fragrance of those now flowering.

PATRICE GIFFORD

The only security for happiness
is to have a mind filled with the love
of the infinite and the eternal.

SPINOZA

Contentment is not the fulfillment
of what you want, but the realization
of how much you already have.

The duty to our neighbor
is part of our duty to God.

JOHN LUBBOCK

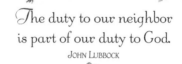

We secure our friends
not by accepting favors
but by doing them.

THUCYDIDES

But, after all, the very best thing in
good talk, and the thing that helps most,
is friendship. How it dissolves the
barriers that divide us, and loosens
all constraint, and diffuses itself
like some fine old cordial

through all the veins of life—
this feeling that we understand
and trust each other, and wish each
other heartily well! Everything into
which it really comes is good.

HENRY VAN DYKE

Some lives,
like evening primroses,
blossom most
beautifully in the
evening of life.

C. E. COWMAN

$\mathcal{F}$riendship is one of the sweetest joys of life. Many might have failed beneath the bitterness of their trial had they not found a friend.

CHARLES H. SPURGEON

*C*heerfulness keeps up a
kind of daylight in the mind
and fills it with a steady
and perpetual serenity.

JOSEPH ADDISON

*A friend
loves at all times,
and a brother is born
for adversity.*

PROVERBS 17:17

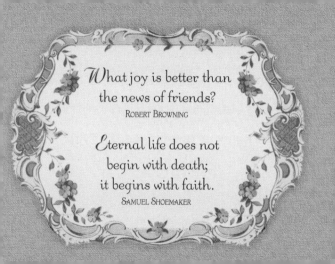

What joy is better than
the news of friends?
ROBERT BROWNING

Eternal life does not
begin with death;
it begins with faith.
SAMUEL SHOEMAKER

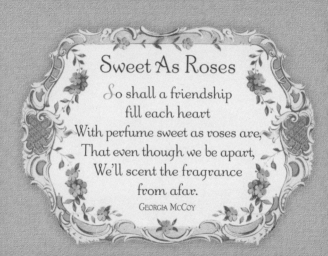

Sweet As Roses

So shall a friendship
fill each heart
With perfume sweet as roses are,
That even though we be apart,
We'll scent the fragrance
from afar.

GEORGIA McCOY

Our great thoughts,
our great affections,
the truths of our life,
never leave us.

WILLIAM MAKEPEACE THACKERAY

Because of a Friend

Because of a friend, life is a little
stronger, fuller, more gracious thing
for the friend's existence, whether he
be near or far. If the friend is close at
hand, that is best; but if he is far
away he still is there to think of, to

wonder about, to hear from, to write
to, to share life and experience with,
to serve, to honor, to admire, to love.

ARTHUR C. BENSON

Though we travel the world over
to find the beautiful,
we must carry it with us
or we find it not.

RALPH WALDO EMERSON

Dear friends,
since God so loved us,
we also ought to
love one another.

1 JOHN 4:11

No people feel closer
or more friendly
than those who
are on the same diet.

ANONYMOUS

*A friend is one
who does not laugh
when you are in
a ridiculous position.*

SIR ARTHUR HELPS

The happiness of life is made up of minute fractions—the little soon forgotten charities of a kiss or smile, a kind look, a heartfelt compliment, and the countless infinitesimals of pleasurable and genial feeling.

SAMUEL TAYLOR COLERIDGE

We Are Different

We are not hen's eggs, or
bananas, or clothespins, to be
counted off by the dozen. Down
to the last detail we are all

different. Everyone has his own
fingerprints. Recognize and
rejoice in that endless variety.

CHARLES R. BROWN

*W*hat a pity that so
many people are living
with so few friends when the
world is full of lonesome
strangers who would
give anything just to be
somebody's friend.

MILO L. ARNOLD

A Friendship Blessing

May our houses and villages
be lighted with the love
God has for each of us.